PRISMS AND LENSES

By the same author

MACHINES

THE ELEMENTS

WORLD BOOK OF GREAT INVENTIONS

FUN WITH MATHEMATICS

THE BOOK OF AMAZING FACTS

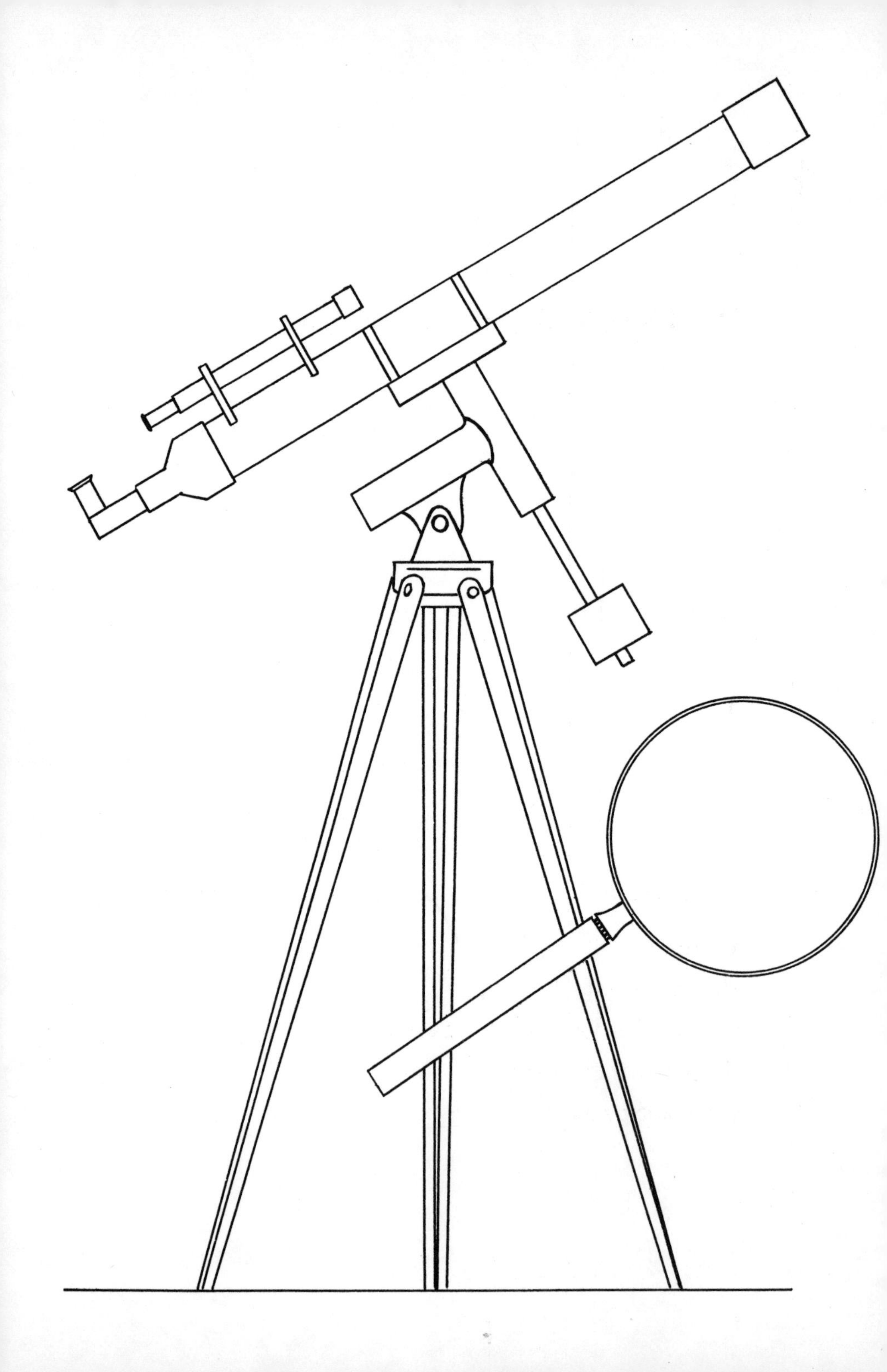

Jerome S. Meyer

PRISMS and LENSES

ILLUSTRATED BY *John Polgreen*

CLEVELAND AND NEW YORK

THE WORLD PUBLISHING COMPANY

Published by The World Publishing Company
2231 West 110th Street, Cleveland 2, Ohio

Published simultaneously in Canada by
Nelson, Foster & Scott Ltd.

Library of Congress Catalog Card Number: 59-11546

COW

To

Nancy, Kate, and Chip Benjamin

PRISMS AND LENSES

IF YOU have ever seen a column of soldiers marching along the avenue, you know how nice and straight that column is and how straight each marching line is. Each soldier keeps abreast of his neighbor in the line, and as long as the lines keep up a steady pace, the entire column moves along the smooth asphalt pavement as straight as an arrow.

Suppose now that the asphalt pavement ends on a slant and becomes a road of cobblestones and mud. What do you think happens to the column as it marches from the smooth to the rough pavement? Naturally, the soldiers can't walk as fast on rough pavement as they can on a smooth one, so the first soldier in the front rank to encounter the roughness has to slow down, although the other soldiers walking on the smooth pavement beside him keep up the regular pace. When the second soldier reaches the rough pavement he, too, slows down. So the pace for the whole line is slowed, until all the soldiers in that line are marching together again on the rough pavement. And as each line comes up to the rough spot it slows down in just the same way. If you were watching this, you would see a definite bending of the column of soldiers as it moves from the smooth to the rough pavement.

Light behaves in much the same way as the marching soldiers. Light travels through air at a constant speed, but as soon as it strikes and passes through some dense medium like water or glass, which are much denser than air, it is slowed down just as the soldiers were when they encountered the rough pavement.

When a beam of light enters water or glass at an angle, it is actually bent like the bending of the column of soldiers. This bending of light is called *refraction.*

This simple experiment will show you how light can be bent. How much it bends depends on your angle of view. Place a fifty cent piece inside a bowl and move away until you can no longer see the coin. Now have a friend slowly and carefully fill the bowl with water so as not to move the coin. You will be able to see the coin from where you are standing.

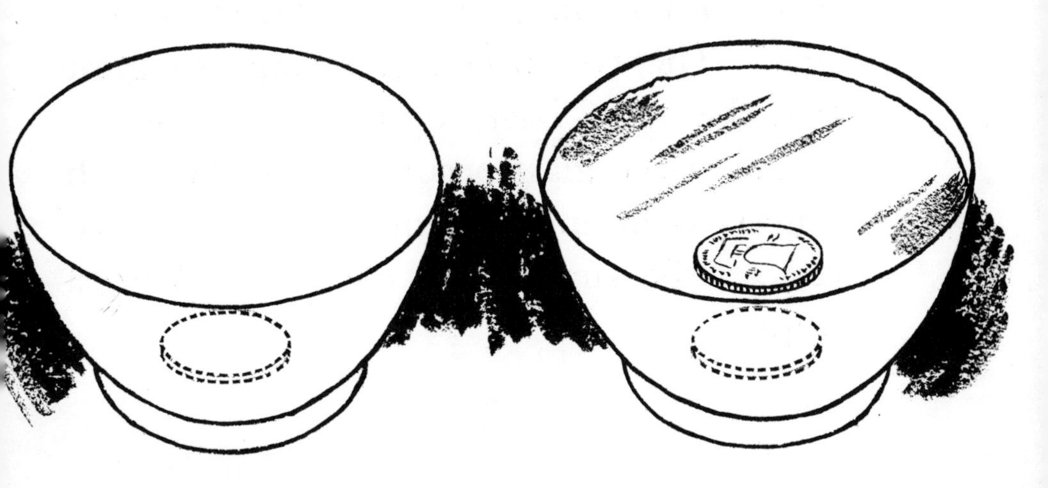

The reason you see the coin now, although you couldn't see it before, is that the reflected light from the coin is actually bent over the top of the bowl. From where you stand, the coin appears to be raised up from the bottom.

Have you ever tried to look through the top of an ordinary glass filled with water to see a coin placed on the other side of the glass? Since glass and water are transparent, you would expect to be able to see through the water in the glass. But you won't be able to see the coin because the other side of the glass (on the inside) becomes an excellent curved mirror which shuts out the light completely. As you look through the top of the water at a sharp angle, your line of sight is bent, and in leaving the glass, it is bent again. The two bendings become so great that the light "backs up on itself," and the inside of the glass becomes a mirror which reflects light and does not transmit it. You can get the same mirror effect by holding a

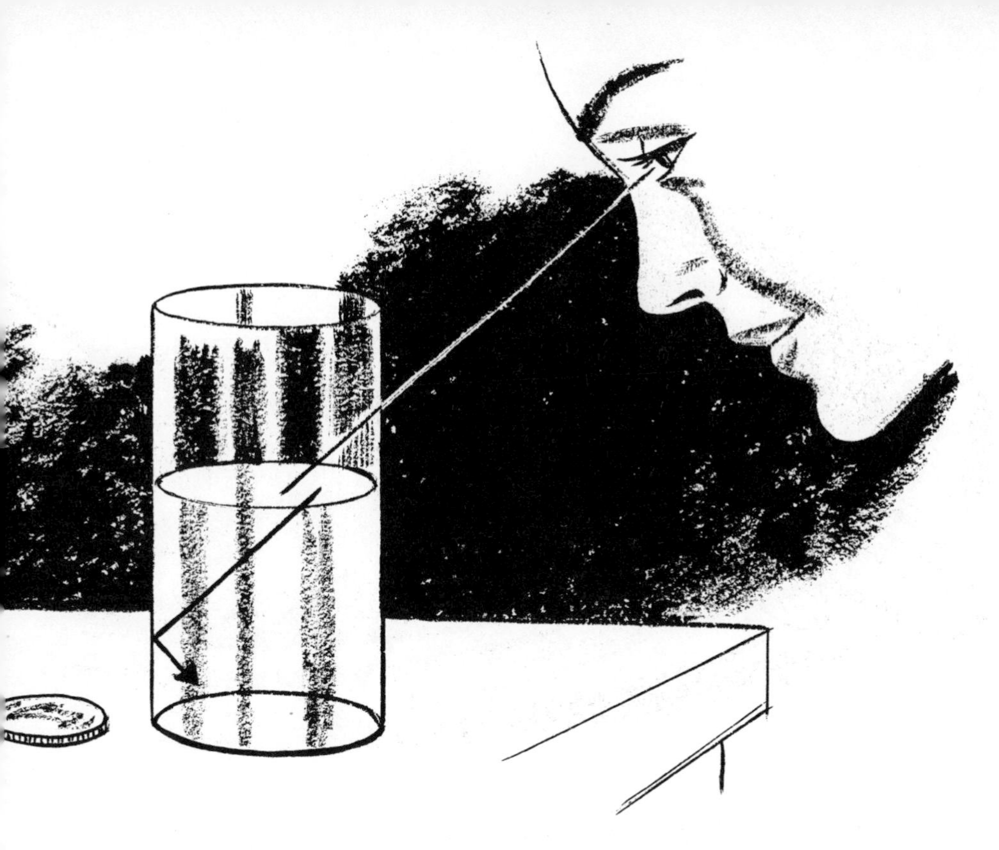

glass of water above your eyes and looking at the underside of the water. It will be a mirror. When light rebounds from any object it strikes, the effect it produces is called *reflection.*

You can perform many experiments with refraction, and some of them will be laughable. If you want to make your hand appear to be half as long as it is and your fingers

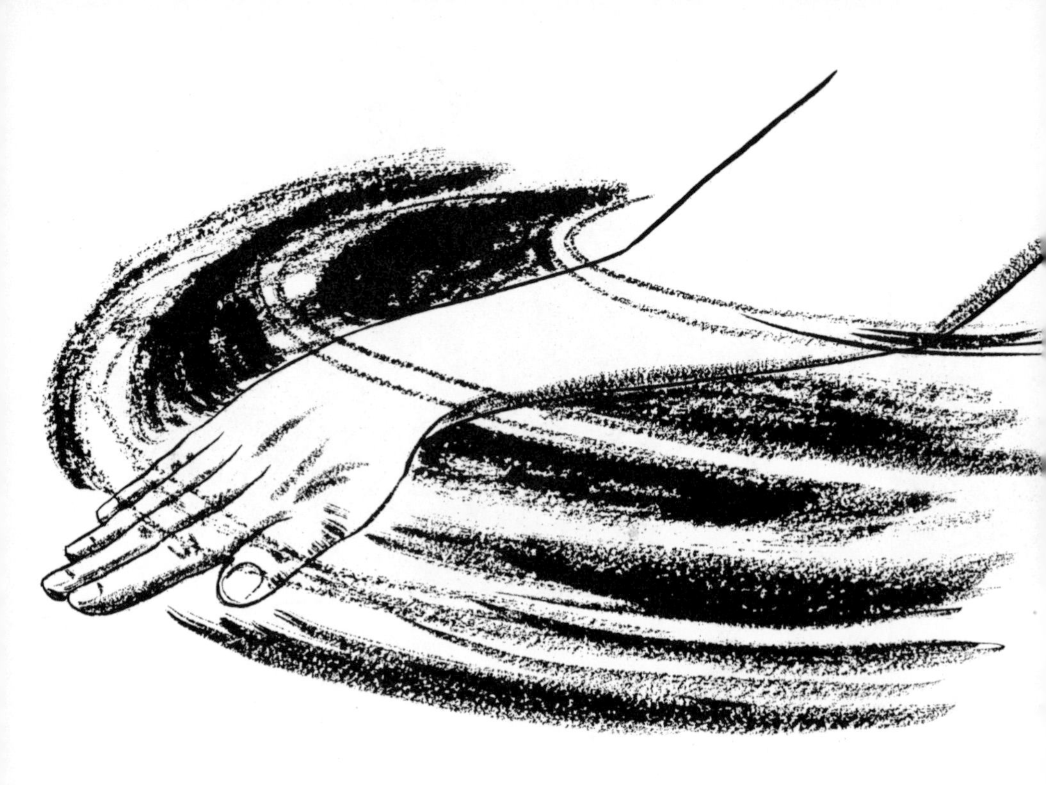

look like little stubs, hold your hand upright under water and view it at an angle.

Not all light that falls on glass or water is refracted at the same angle, however. Here is another experiment that shows more about how light is refracted.

Place a cube of glass or transparent plastic on a newspaper and look directly down on it. The print will appear to be raised up from the rest of the paper. Now, if you move away and look over the top of the cube at an angle, you will still see the print and its reflection on the side of the cube. This time the print will be raised up much higher than before. And the next time you look at a glass tank of water containing fish, note how you can see around the corner of the tank. Because

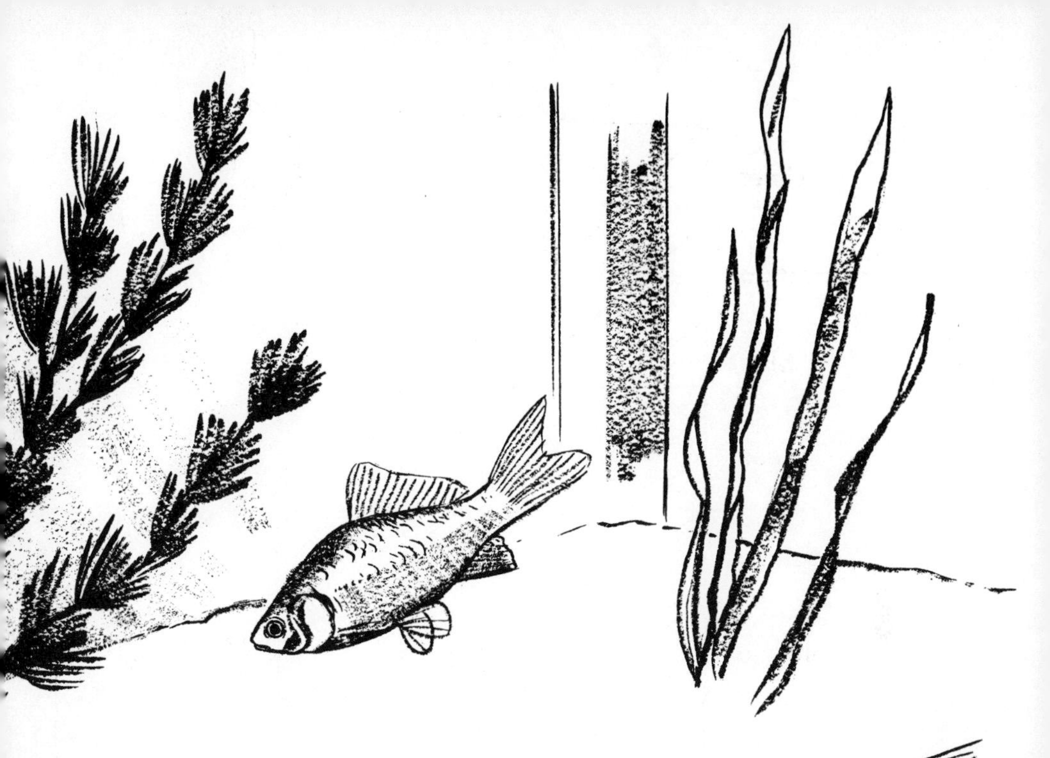

of the great angle of refraction of the light as it comes to you through the water, you will be able to see at the same time the same fish in the side of the tank as you see in the front of the tank.

This spreading of light by differences of refraction is called *dispersion.* Although all light is refracted or bent when it passes slantingly through water or glass or any other

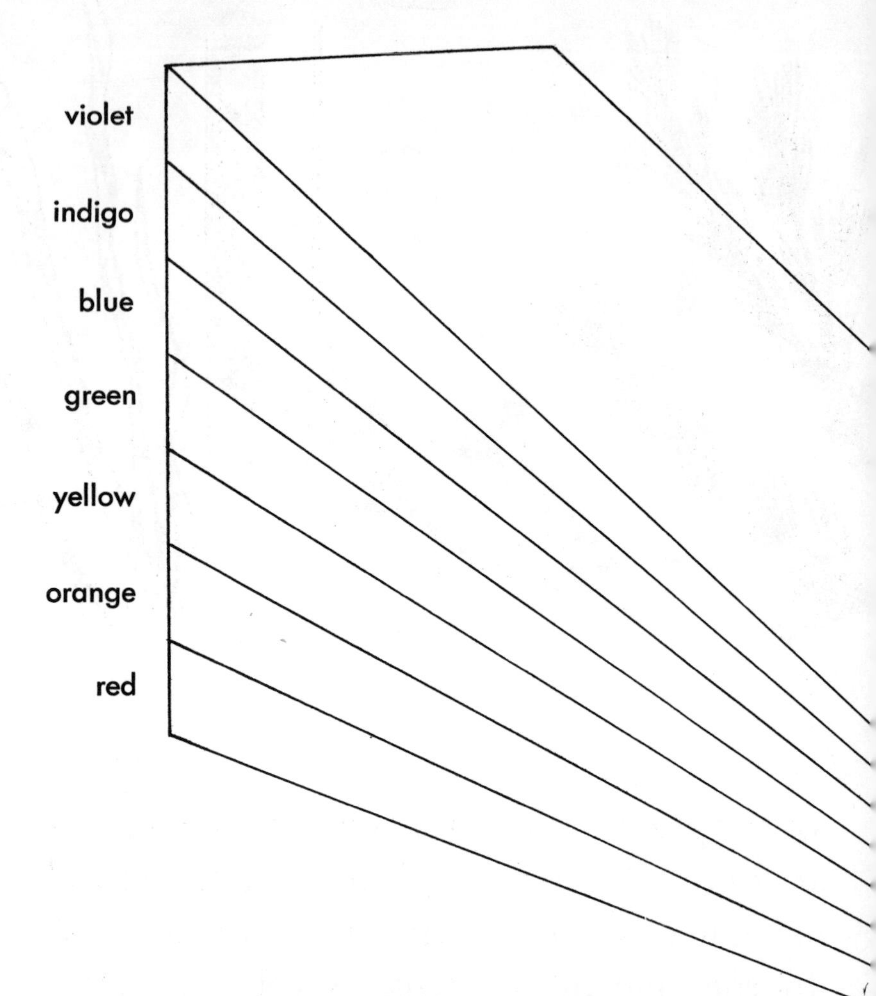

dense transparent medium, it is bent in various degrees depending on the angle of view.

Colors, too, are caused by the refraction of light, depending on the angle at which it strikes a prism. There are very slight differences of angle for different colors. That is why it is possible to break up a beam of light into a band of color like a rainbow with a prism.

A prism is simply a piece of glass or transparent plastic material in the shape of a solid triangle with equal sides. This is the simplest form of prism, but all prisms, no matter how

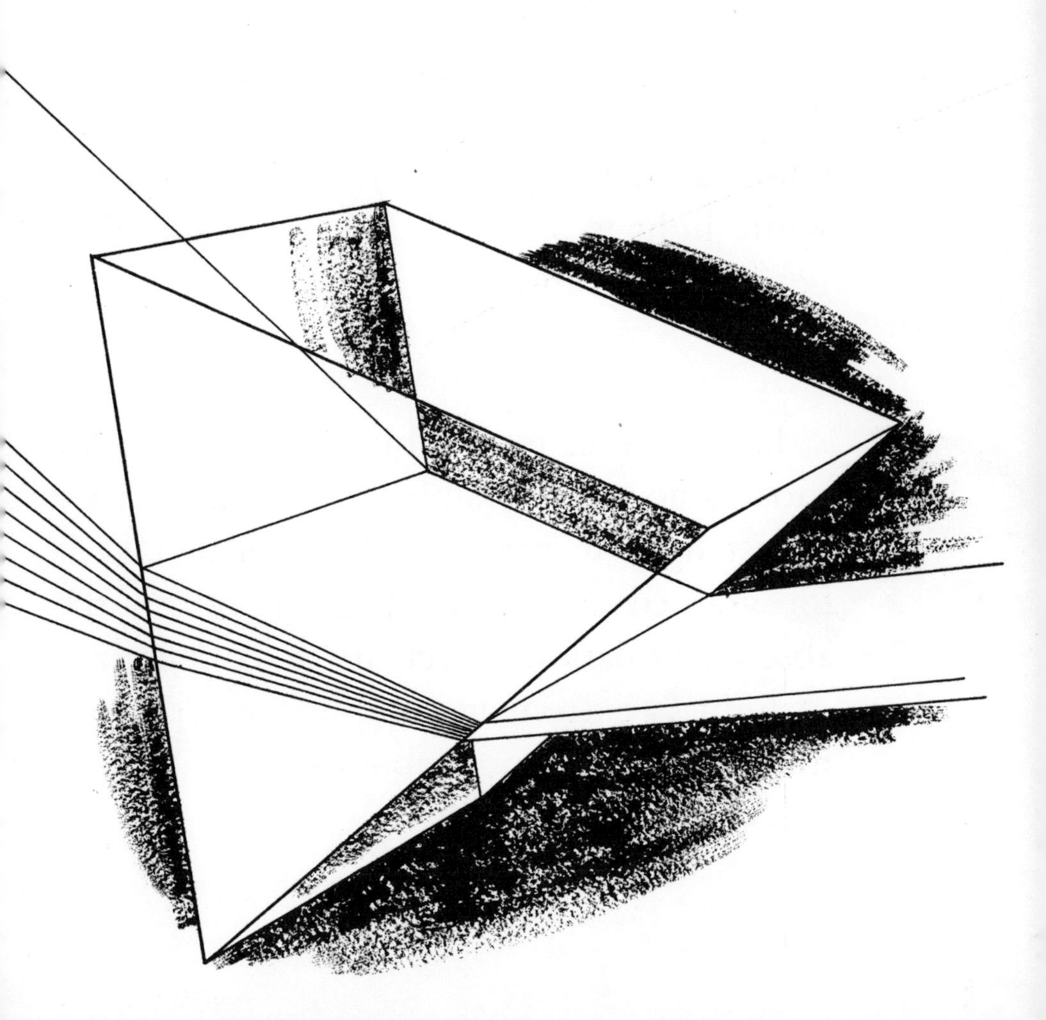

complex, are combinations of solid equal triangles. When a beam of white light is sent through a prism slantingly, a remarkable thing takes place. The beam is bent toward the base of the prism when it enters it, but on leaving it, the light is refracted at a number of slightly different angles. It breaks up into a band of vivid color consisting of red, orange, yellow, green, blue, indigo, and violet. This band of colors is called a *spectrum.* These colors are all part of white light, and when white light is broken up in this manner we get the spectrum.

WHAT IS LIGHT?

Light makes it possible for us to see, for most objects are visible to us because they reflect light to our eyes. Most of us take it for granted and define light as merely the absence of darkness. Yet the exact definition of light is extremely complex, and there is much we don't know about it.

In your room at this very minute there are hundreds of different invisible waves, somewhat like water waves, with as many different vibrations. These waves, which are both electrical and magnetic and are called electromagnetic waves, fill all the space where you are. You cannot see them or hear them or feel them, and you would never know they were there until you turned on your radio or TV. As these invisible waves get shorter and shorter, there are more of them in a given distance; and so they vibrate faster and faster until there comes a time when they can actually be felt in the form of heat waves.

As these heat waves grow shorter and their vibrations get faster, you not only can feel them, but you begin to see them, and they turn into light waves. So light may be defined roughly as visible radiations or vibrations in space. Unlike radio or heat waves of which they are a part, they are so small and they vibrate so quickly that they affect

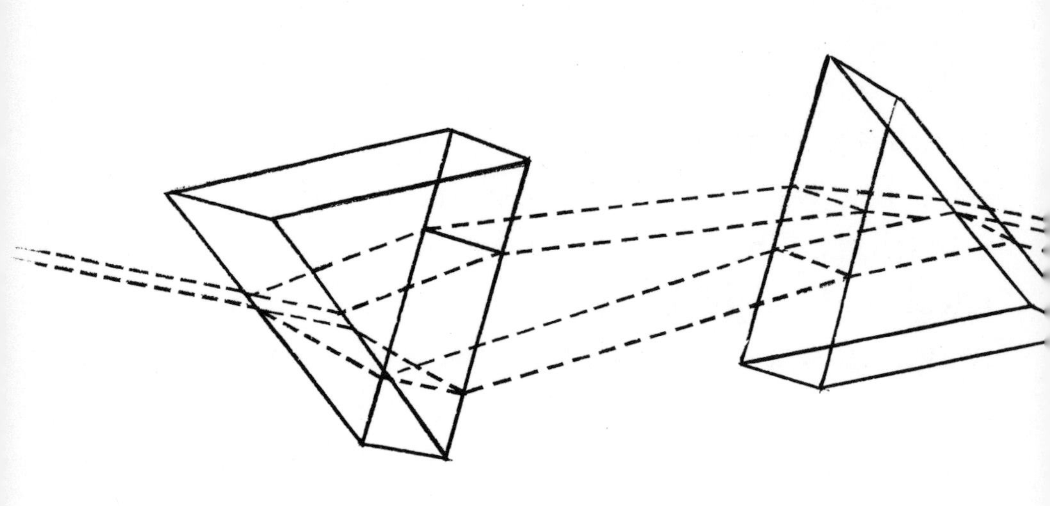

our optic nerves and thus enable us to see.

Sir Isaac Newton was the first to investigate the nature of light. He used a glass prism to break up the white light of the sun into the rainbow colors and then sent these colors back into a second prism to produce white light once again. This started him thinking, and he asked himself such questions as: "Why is light reflected when it strikes a shiny surface like a mirror, and why is it refracted when it passes through a dense medium like glass?" "And why does white

Sir Isaac Newton

light break up into beautiful colors when it passes through a glass prism?" After weeks of careful experiments and intensive study, Newton suggested that light is nothing more than billions and trillions of invisible particles, called *corpuscles,* shot out at terrific speed from a luminous body like so many invisible bullets from a machine gun. When these corpuscles strike a mirror or other shiny surface they bounce right back like tiny rubber balls, and when they pass through a dense medium they are slowed down. Newton's corpuscular theory explained reflection and refraction perfectly, but it did not account for the colors in white light after being sent through a prism.

A much more satisfactory explanation of light was given in the year 1678 by the Dutch scientist Christian Huygens. Huygens explained light as a wave motion. He said that light travels in waves somewhat like water waves or sound waves, and this accounted for all the different ways in which light be-

Christian Huygens experimenting with an "aerial telescope"

haves. It proved to be such a perfect theory that it captured the imagination of scientists the world over and for more than 150 years the *wave theory of light,* as it was called, was accepted as fully explaining the behavior of light even though it did not explain what light really is.

But as perfect as the wave theory seems to be, there is one important thing that it cannot account for. We know very well that there cannot be a wave motion without some

medium to conduct it. Without air there could be no sound, because sound is a vibration which disturbs the air and produces waves which travel just the way ripples travel on a still lake when you throw a stone into it. Sound, then, is a wave motion in air. And if light (like sound) travels in waves, it must have some medium like air to conduct it.

Now we know that there is no air or any other medium between the earth and the distant stars. The universe is a vast void of cold, black airless space; yet we can go out on any clear night and see stars that are trillions of billions of miles away. How does the light

from these stars get to us if light is a wave motion and there is nothing to conduct it to the earth?

Scientists puzzled over this question for years until someone devised a medium to transmit light, calling it the "ether." The ether was supposed to fill all the space throughout the entire universe; and by some unexplained manner, light traveled through it just as sound travels through air. The ether theory satisfied scientists for twenty-five years until a brilliant Scottish physicist named James Clerk Maxwell started to question its

existence. Maxwell demanded proof of the existence of the ether. He said that science cannot accept any idea without proof, and he questioned whether there was an ether at all. Other scientists began to doubt the existence of the ether, too; and in 1887, several years after Maxwell died, two young physicists started experimenting to prove, once and for all, whether or not there was such a medium as the ether.

It was supposed that as the earth goes whizzing around the central sun at eighteen miles a second and rotates on its axis at a thousand miles an hour it would naturally "swish" some of this ether around with it, just as a fast express train creates a heavy wind as it passes by. After more than twenty of the most complicated and exacting experiments were repeated over and over again, no ether drift was detected and scientists had to conclude that there is no ether.

As the result of this famous experiment a

Albert Einstein

new theory of light was needed, and the greatest scientific minds of the world started concentrating on this difficult problem. The two scientists who contributed most to producing the present theory of light were Max Planck and Albert Einstein. According to them, light is made up of tiny bundles of energy, called *photons,* traveling with enormous velocity from luminous bodies. This would seem to support Newton's original theory about the corpuscles, but it went much farther. It showed that in addition to traveling in waves, this energy also had mass, or weight. We cannot think of energy without thinking of motion and we can't think of motion without thinking of something moving. Energy always has to do with a body in motion, no matter how large or how small, and the faster the motion, or velocity, the greater the energy.

The velocity of light is more than 186,000 miles per second, and since it is a form of energy, it has some weight even though it cannot be measured by any known scale. This is what Einstein, the greatest scientist of this century, wrote: "A beam of light carries energy and energy has mass. But every mass is attracted by a gravitational field and a beam of light will bend in this gravitational field exactly as a body would if thrown horizontally with a speed equal to that of light."

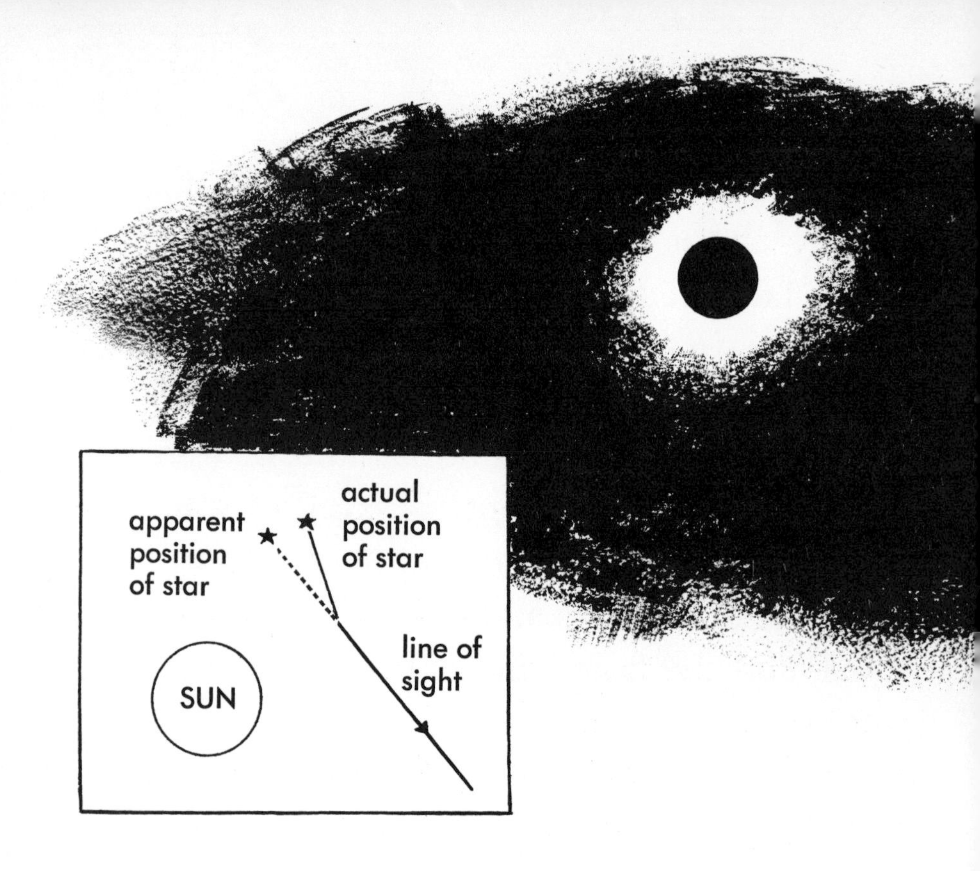

Light then consists of bundles of invisible vibrating electrical and magnetic particles traveling in waves through space like billions of tiny rockets. Having weight or mass, it is attracted by gravity. This was demonstrated by Einstein with the aid of the sun eclipse of 1905 when the light from a star passed close to the sun and was bent by the sun's gravitational pull.

Many people do not realize that Einstein's study of light and the speed of light form the basis for his famous Theory of Relativity, which revolutionized scientific thinking and made possible many wonders of modern physics, including television and electronic calculating machines. And out of his study of the behavior of light and his conclusions about its complex nature came the new age of atomic energy which opens up hundreds of new ideas for the benefit and comfort of all of us.

So, you see, when we speak of light we speak of something that is not easy to define. An accurate explanation of its nature is extremely difficult. Light actually does travel through space in waves, and because it has mass, inconceivably tiny as it may be, it does not need a medium like air or water to conduct it. So we can consider it to be a wave motion like the waves on the ocean. The distance from the top of one wave to the top of the next one is called the *wave length,* and the

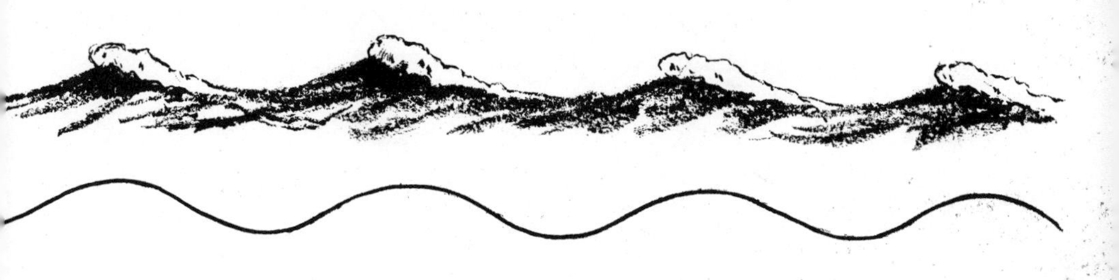

number of these wave lengths or waves that pass a given point in a second is called the *frequency.* In radio the different stations broadcast sound by sending sound waves on a carrier wave of a certain frequency—so many thousands of vibrations (called *kilocycles*) per second. By turning the dial on your set you tune in on a particular frequency; Station WOR in New York has a frequency of 710 kilocycles or 710,000 vibrations per second; other stations have other frequencies.

The wave length of color in light is incredibly small: not more than a few hundred millionths of an inch. The frequency, however, is extremely high: several billion vibrations per second. The longer the wave length, the lower the frequency; and the shorter the wave length, the higher the frequency. Red

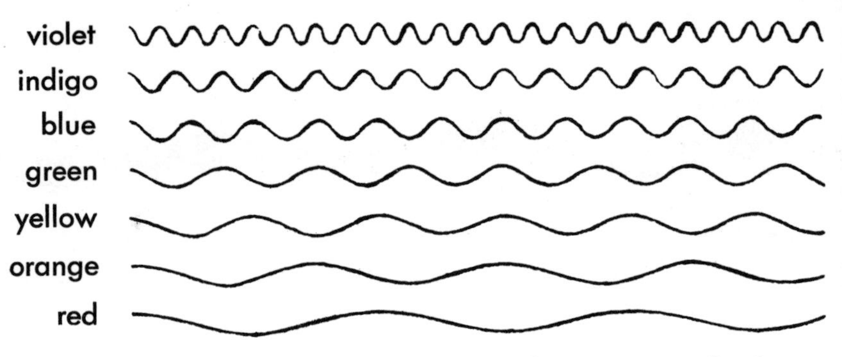

light has the longest wave length and the lowest frequency, and that is why it can be seen from a great distance. Violet light has the shortest wave length and the highest frequency and is the first color to vanish as the distance from it increases. All colors in between red and violet have wave lengths and frequencies that vary accordingly.

So color in light is nothing more than an inconceivably rapid vibration (called frequency) of incredibly small waves (called wave lengths), and when all the colors are combined they instantly turn back into the white light from which they are produced.

The light from the sun is almost pure white, and the spectrum that results from sending that light through a prism gives each particular color its true value. No color seems to be more prevalent or intense than any other.

White light is not the only source of light that produces a spectrum. The elements, which are the basic particles of which everything in the universe is composed, also give off light when heated sufficiently. Each element (there are ninety-two natural ones) has its own particular light, and the color of that light determines the element just as surely as a man's fingerprints determine his identity. So when light from one of the elements is sent through a prism, the spectrum that results is not the same as the spectrum made by the white light of the sun. The element sodium, for example, gives a bright yellow flame; the element lithium gives a bright red flame; the element copper gives a green flame. Naturally, these colored lights produce spectra of a special color. The yellow band in the spectrum from sodium light will be much more vivid and much stronger than the other

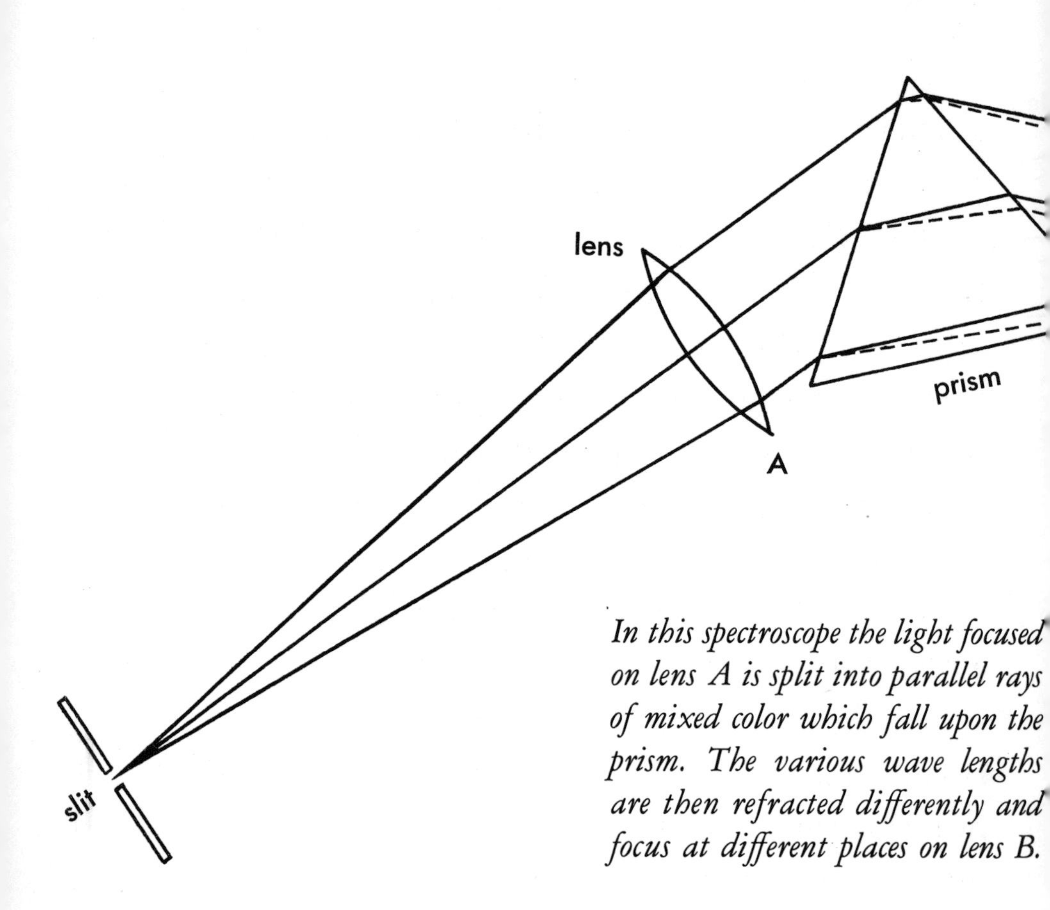

In this spectroscope the light focused on lens A is split into parallel rays of mixed color which fall upon the prism. The various wave lengths are then refracted differently and focus at different places on lens B.

colors. The red band in the spectrum from lithium light will be much more vivid and much stronger than the other colors. The green band in the spectrum from copper will be much more vivid and stronger than the other colors. And this is true for other ele-

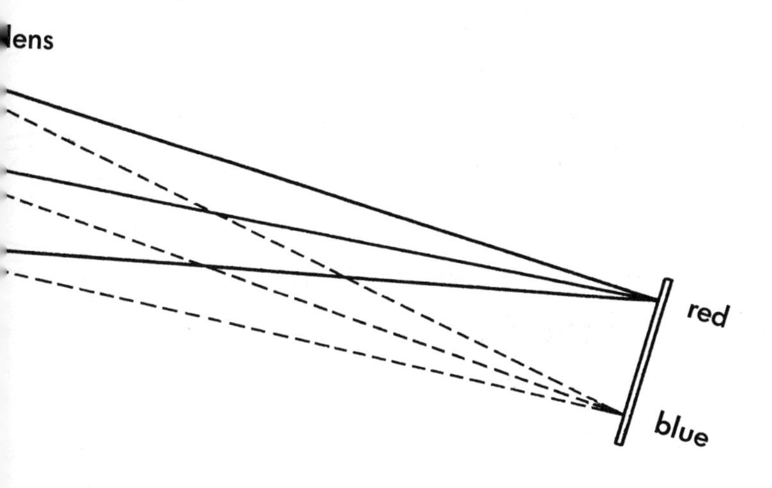

ments, too, according to the color of the flame they give off when heated.

The instrument used in analyzing the spectra of different elements and substances is called a *spectroscope.* In its simplest form it consists of a glass prism inside a cylinder with a slit in it at one end and a lens at the other. Light from the element or substance enters the slit and is sent in straight lines through a prism where it is refracted into and through a small telescopic lens to be examined by the eye or photographed by a camera.

By intensifying the light from distant

planets and stars and sending it through a carefully constructed glass prism inside the spectroscope, astronomers can tell by the degrees of intensity of the different colors in the spectrum, the make-up of the sun or star or planet and the different elements that are present there. That is how we know that the atmosphere of Venus is a gas called carbon dioxide. That is how we know that Mars has a very tiny amount of oxygen in its extremely rare atmosphere. And that is how we know a great deal about our own sun and the distant suns which we call stars. A long and intensive

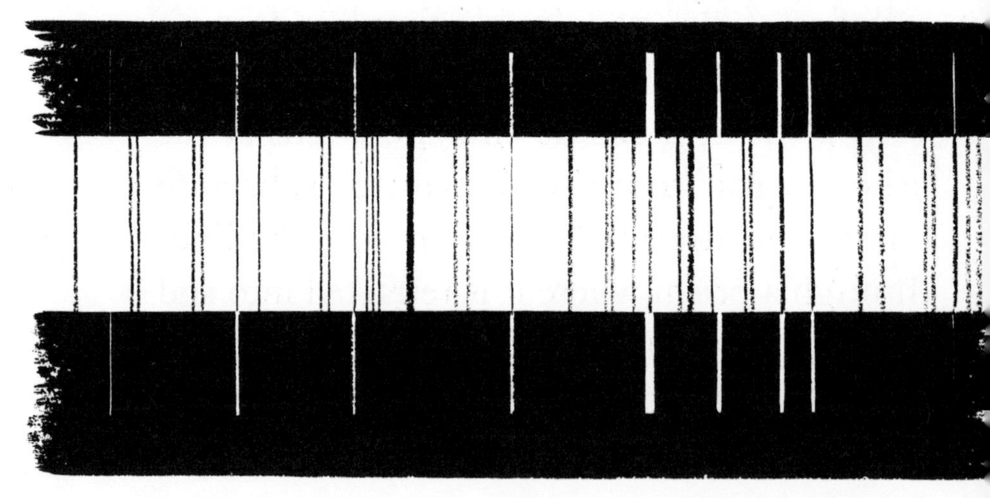

The intensity of colors in a typical stellar spectrum analysis are registered on a spectrograph.

study of the composition of stars is called *spectrum analysis.* The prism is very important in spectrum analysis.

In addition to the ninety-two natural elements, each of which produces a definite and different spectrum, scientists have actually created ten man-made elements in the laboratory. These elements play a very important part in atomic science today, and their nature and composition are determined to a great extent through spectrum analysis.

Spectroscopes have other uses, too. The purity of different metals and other substances used in industry can easily be determined by means of a spectroscope. And this is very important. Steel, for example, loses strength if it has impurities in it. Through spectrum analysis it can be tested to make sure there are no impurities. The spectroscope is also used in police laboratories for identifying the composition of unknown objects which may give clues to solving crimes.

Prisms refract light in such a way that it breaks up into colors. Lenses also refract light by changing the direction of light rays, bringing them to a focus. In its simplest form, a lens is merely a piece of round glass with either one or two curved surfaces that refract light. It is one of man's most wonderful and most important inventions.

The purpose of a lens when focused on a

picture or scene is to make or help make an image of that picture or scene. Most times the image is upside down and smaller than the scene. You can see a good example of how a lens works by holding a reading glass between the light from a window and a clean sheet of white paper. Move the paper back and forth until you see a perfect image of the window, upside down on the paper.

So vital is the lens to all of us that without it we would be totally blind. The lens of the eye is made of a jellylike substance as clear as the clearest crystal. It is located directly behind the opening in the iris, or pupil, of the eye and acts in exactly the same way that the lens in a camera acts. When light rays from an object pass through the lens, a tiny image of that object is produced on the back of the eyeball known as the retina. The retina is a mass of millions of tiny nerve fibers connected to a large nerve called the optic nerve which immediately transfers the image to the brain. The brain automatically projects the image right side up and we are able to see. Sight, one of our most precious possessions, would

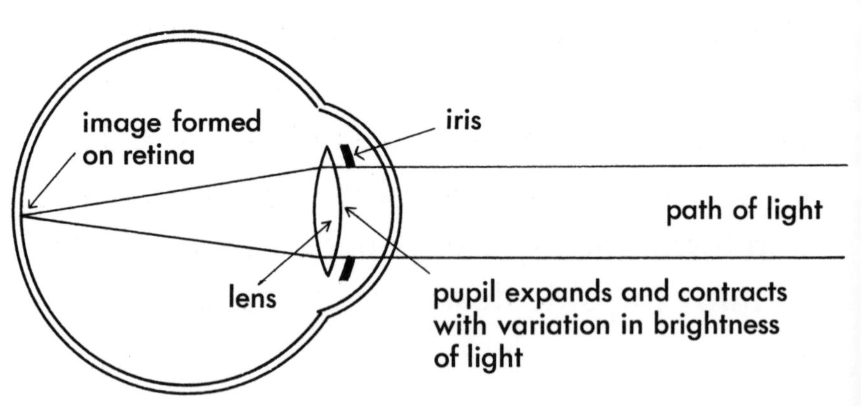

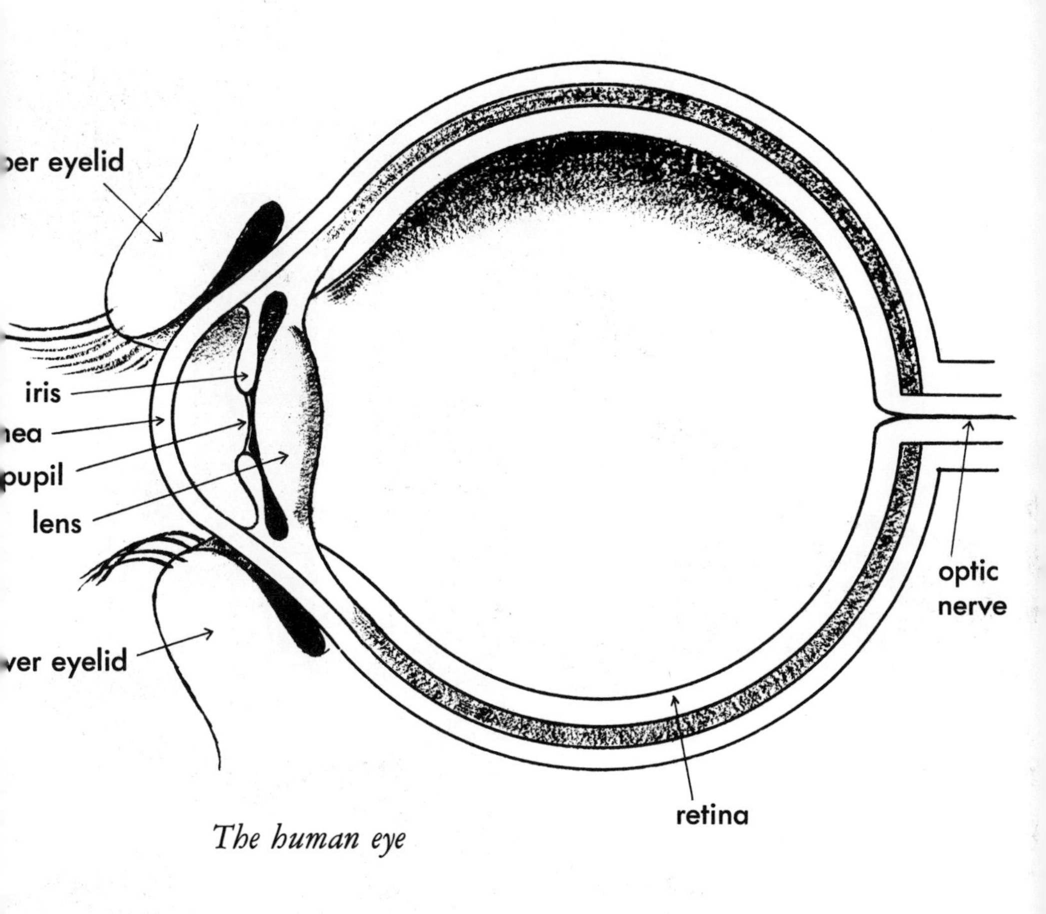

The human eye

be impossible without the lens, which in this case is made of clear gelatin. So marvelous is the human eye that all the most complicated and remarkable inventions of man put together seem as commonplace as an ordinary pin by comparison.

Eyeglasses are lenses which people use to help them see better when their own eyes are weak or imperfect. Telescopes have lenses that make it possible to see people or objects at a great distance. Microscopes have lenses that allow us to see objects that are too small to be seen by the human eye. Cameras have lenses that allow us to reproduce images on paper or film. Without the lens there could

Hans Lippershey

be no pictures of any kind in books or magazines or newspapers. There could be no movies or TV, no microscopes so vital to curing diseases, no telescopes so important in astronomy, no real accuracy in surveying or building construction and, indeed, no vision for any of us.

As important as the lens is, its inventor is unknown. As far as we know, it was first used by an Italian named Amati of Florence in the year 1285. He noticed that he could see to read much better by looking through glass that was curved in a particular manner. An-

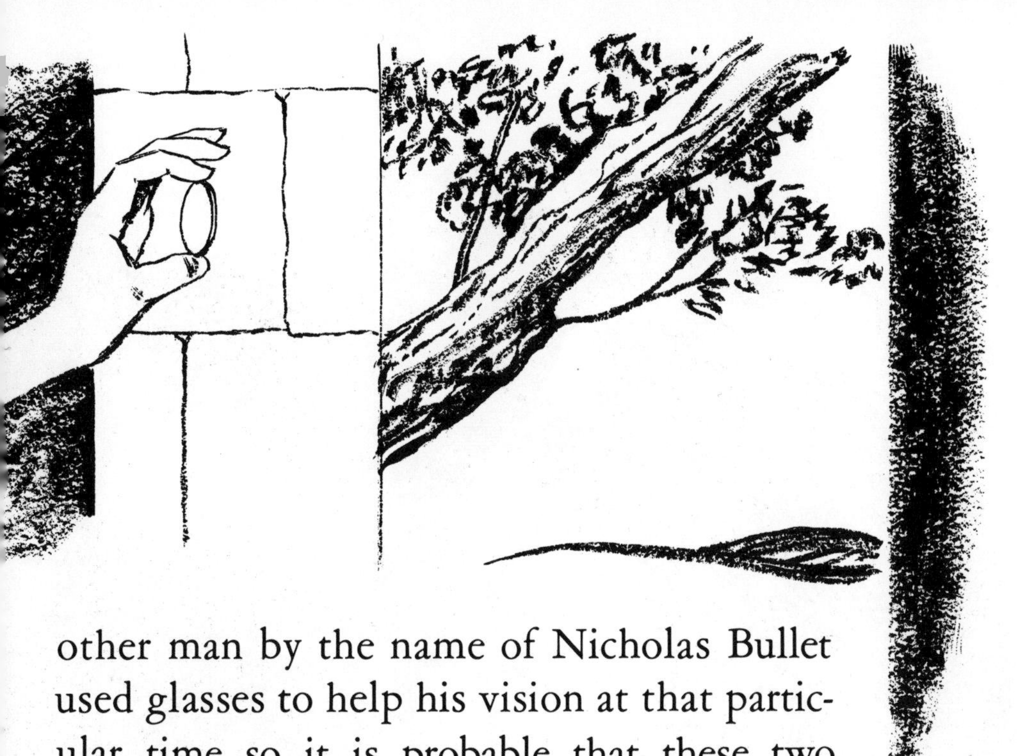

other man by the name of Nicholas Bullet used glasses to help his vision at that particular time so it is probable that these two men started the science of optics and invented eyeglasses. It wasn't long before people started wearing eyeglasses to improve their vision, and soon there were oculists and opticians all over Europe. Many years later an optician by the name of Hans Lippershey, who was testing the strength of two eyeglass lenses, was startled to see that when one lens was brought in front of the other, distant objects suddenly appeared to be very near. This accidental dis-

Galileo

covery produced the first crude telescope, which was later perfected by the great Italian scientist Galileo. Galileo made the very first telescope that was practical to use. Through it he was able to see the satellites, or moons, of the planet Jupiter for the first time.

The microscope was invented around 1600 and has done more to save human lives than any other invention. Whenever we think of a microscope and how it has made it possible for us to conquer many diseases, one name stands out above all others: the name of the

Dutch scientist Anton van Leeuwenhoek. He was the first man to examine rain water under his homemade microscope and discover the thousands of tiny creatures called microbes swimming around in it. As these microbes are invisible to the naked eye, no one knew before that they existed. Leeuwenhoek's discovery was one of the most important in all science, because by learning about microbes we learned how diseases are caused; and by studying the habits and nature of microbes through the microscope, great scientists like Louis Pasteur showed how to kill them or make them so harmless that most diseases can be prevented. One way to kill the invisible germs is to scald them, and that is why doctors put instruments in boiling water

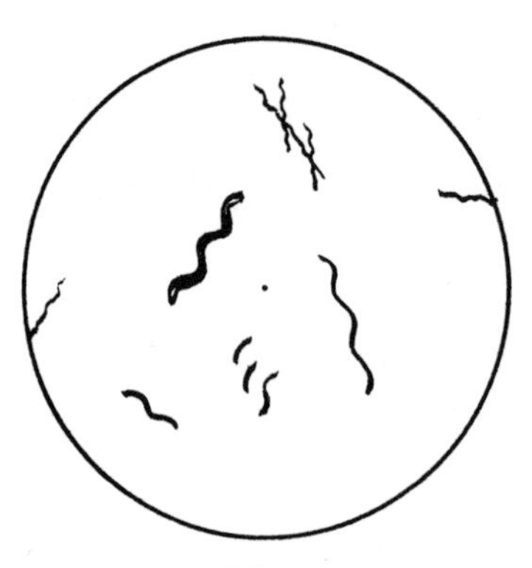

spiral bacteria
(spirilla)

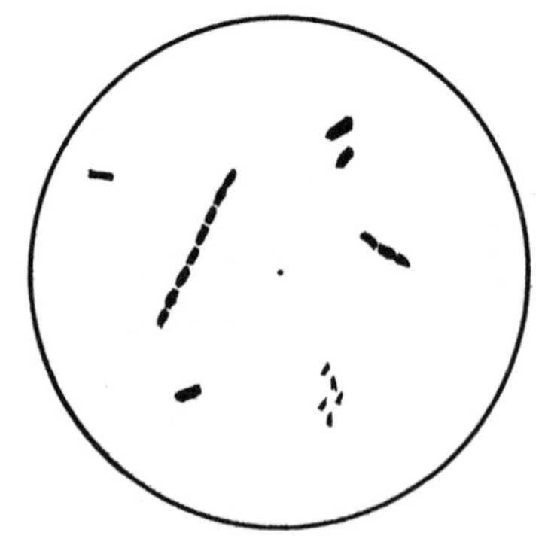

rod-shaped bacteria
(bacilli)

Anton van Leeuwenhoek

before performing an operation. The process of killing microbes and germs by boiling or scalding them is called sterilizing.

THE DIFFERENT KINDS OF LENSES

There are many different kinds of lenses, but all of them are divided into two groups: *convex* and *concave.* It is easy to see the difference between these groups by looking at an ordinary spoon. The outside of the spoon has a rounded surface and is called convex. The inside of the spoon is hollow and is called concave. These two new words are used continually with reference to lenses. The word *convex* means "curved out," like the outside surface of a ball. The word *concave* means "curved in," like the inside of a hollow rubber ball.

In a convex lens the glass surface is thicker in the middle than at the edges, and curves out. It causes light rays to draw together into focus. It usually produces images upside

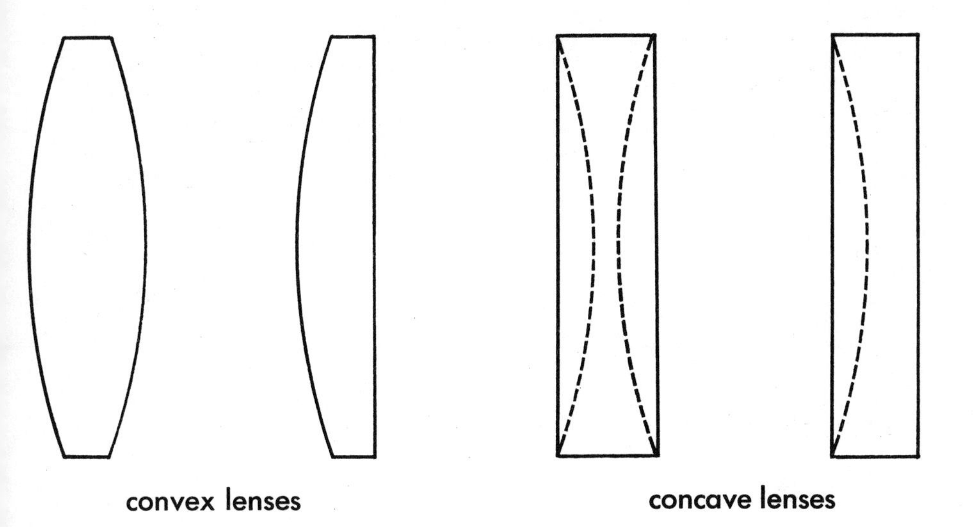

down (called *real images*), but it can produce an enlarged image that is right side up (called a *virtual image*).

In a concave lens the glass surface is thinner in the middle than at the edges, and curves in. It spreads light rays apart (diverging rays), and the image always appears right side up and greatly reduced.

When one side of a lens is flat and the other side is curved out or in, we have a *plano-convex* or a *plano-concave* lens.

In a double convex lens both surfaces

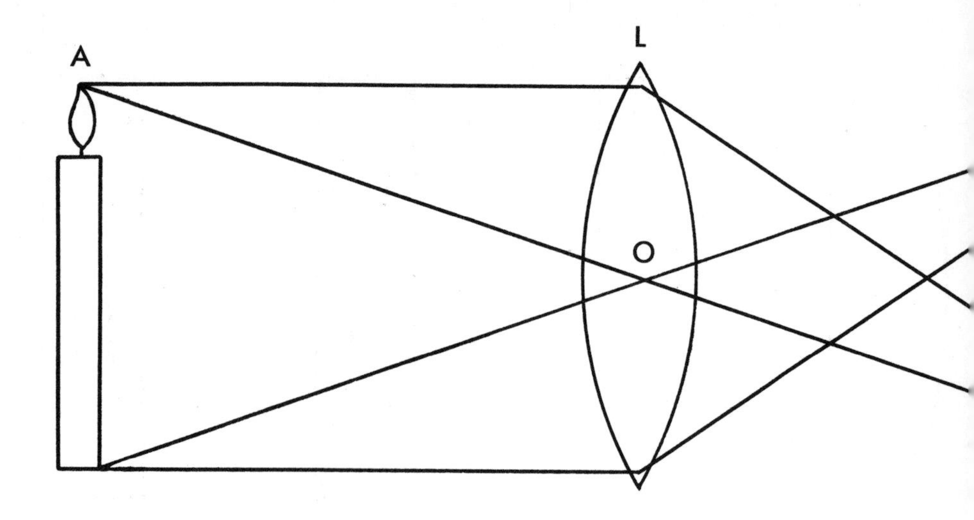

curve out; in a double concave lens both surfaces curve in.

Now let's see how the double convex lens enlarges and reduces objects and how the light behaves when passing through it.

L is a double convex lens and A is a candle a short distance from it. The light rays from the candle which strike the lens at its thickest part (O) pass straight through the lens and are not bent. All other rays, striking the lens at its thinner parts, are bent at angles according to their distance from the center. The image is formed where the bent rays

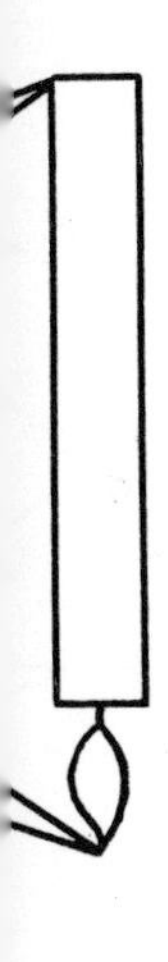

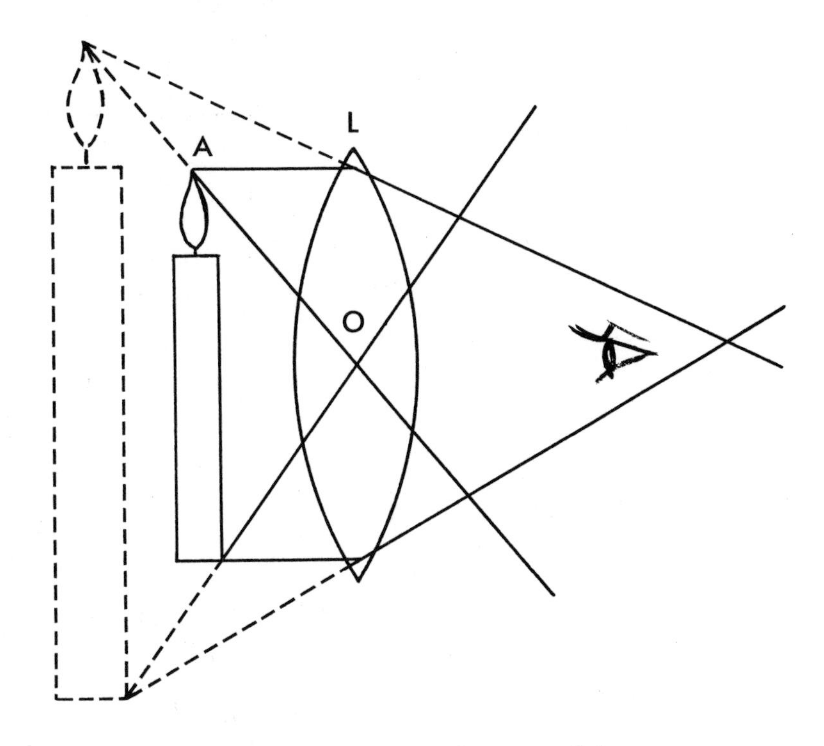

meet the straight rays. Since it is a real image, it is upside down. The point at which the bent rays meet and pass is called the *focus.*

Now see what happens when you look through the lens at an object near the other side of it. Suppose the lens is so close to your eye that the focus (where all the bent rays meet) is behind you. Just as before, the rays are bent according to their distance from the

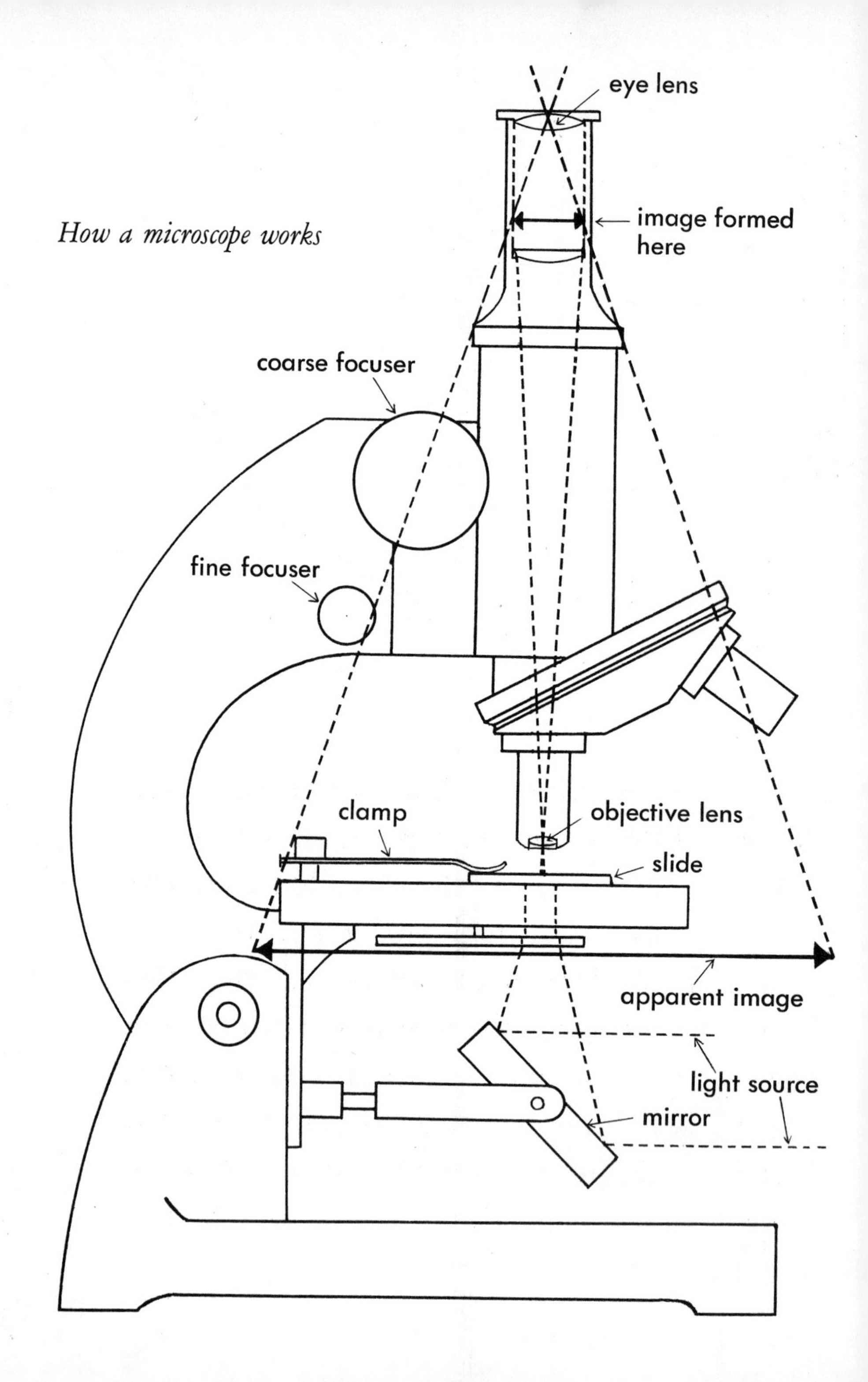

How a microscope works

center O and all rays that pass through the center remain straight, but this time the bent rays do not meet; they travel backward until they meet the straight rays and a very large image is formed. This image is not upside down and is a virtual image because it is not formed in space. By using another double convex lens we can make the image still larger. That is the principle of the microscope.

The microscope consists of a powerful double convex lens. When it is placed close to a very tiny object, it magnifies it greatly. The image of this tiny object, greatly enlarged, is sent up the tube of the microscope where another powerful double convex lens enlarges it again. In this way microbes and germs that are invisible to the naked eye are clearly seen and studied. They are always seen by transmitted light—a very bright light sent through the glass slide on which they are placed from below.

The double convex lens, combined with

other lenses, is also used in the camera. In principle, a camera is simply a black box with a double convex lens at one end and a film that is extremely sensitive to light at the other. The lens forms an image of the object to be photographed on the film. If the light transmitted through the lens is bright, the film it strikes is black; if no light is transmitted to the film, it is clear. The developed film is just the reverse of the actual scene. All the light parts in the original scene are dark on the film, and all the dark parts in the original scene are light on the film. This is called a negative. By placing the negative

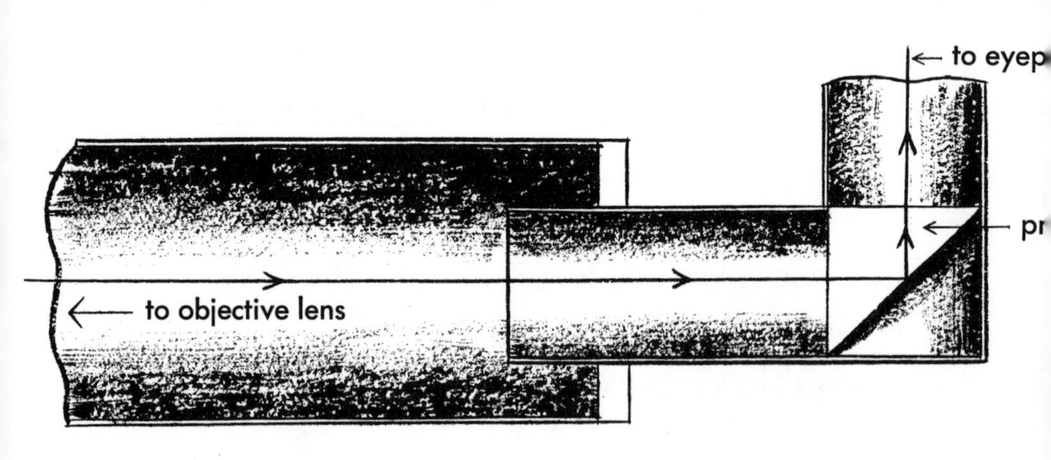

A prism is used in a refracting telescope to bend the light at right angles in order to increase viewing comfort.

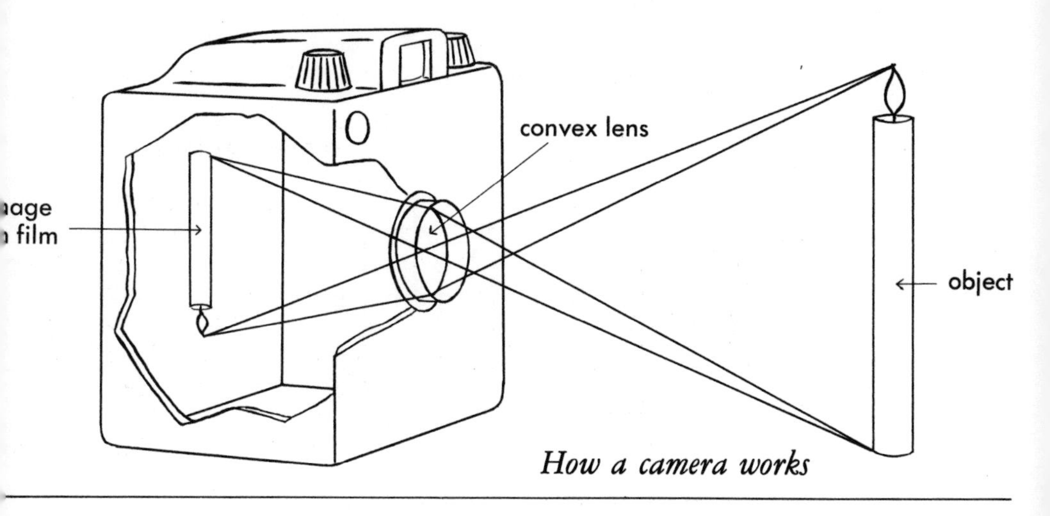

How a camera works

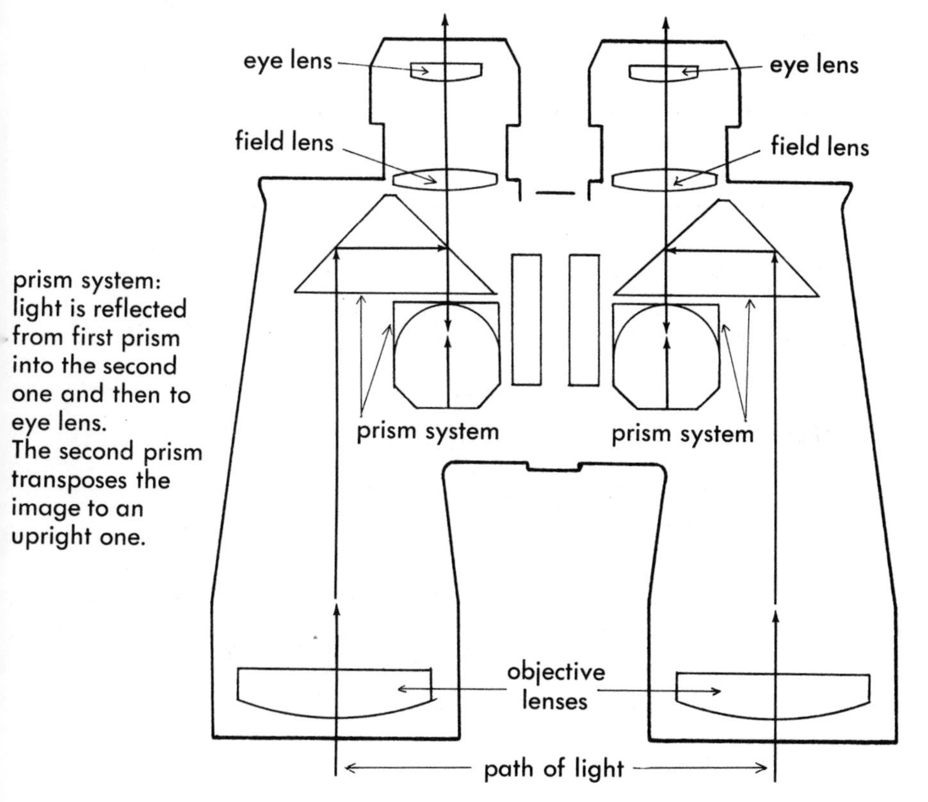

How binoculars work

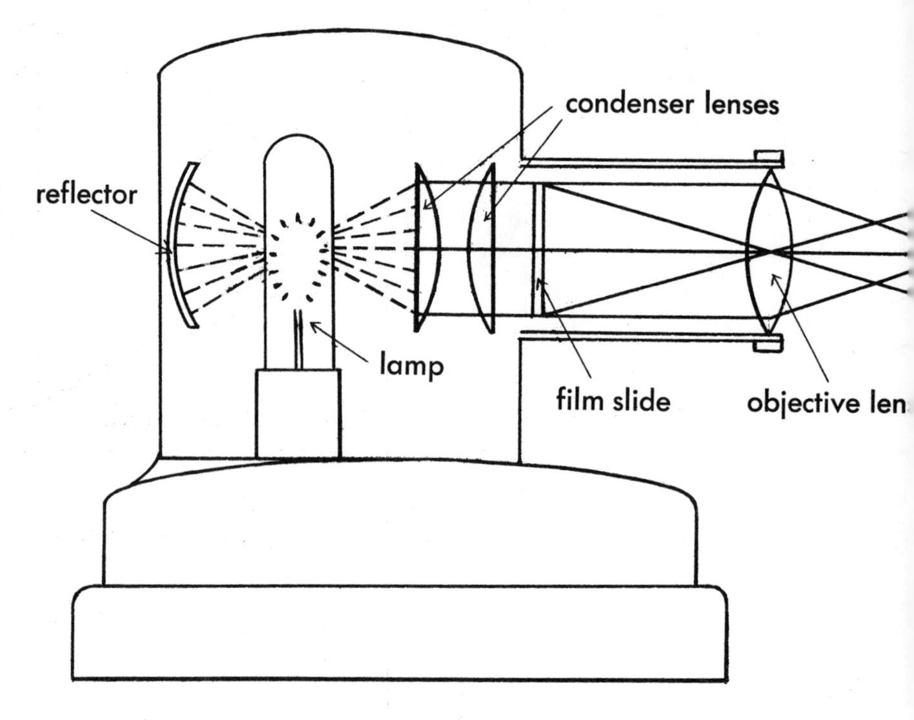

over light-sensitive paper and exposing it to bright light, the negative is again reversed and becomes a positive, or true picture of the original scene. The projecting lantern, which makes movies possible, works in just the opposite way. In the camera the object which the lens records is at a distance from the lens and the image it creates is near-by; in the projecting lantern the object (film or slide) is

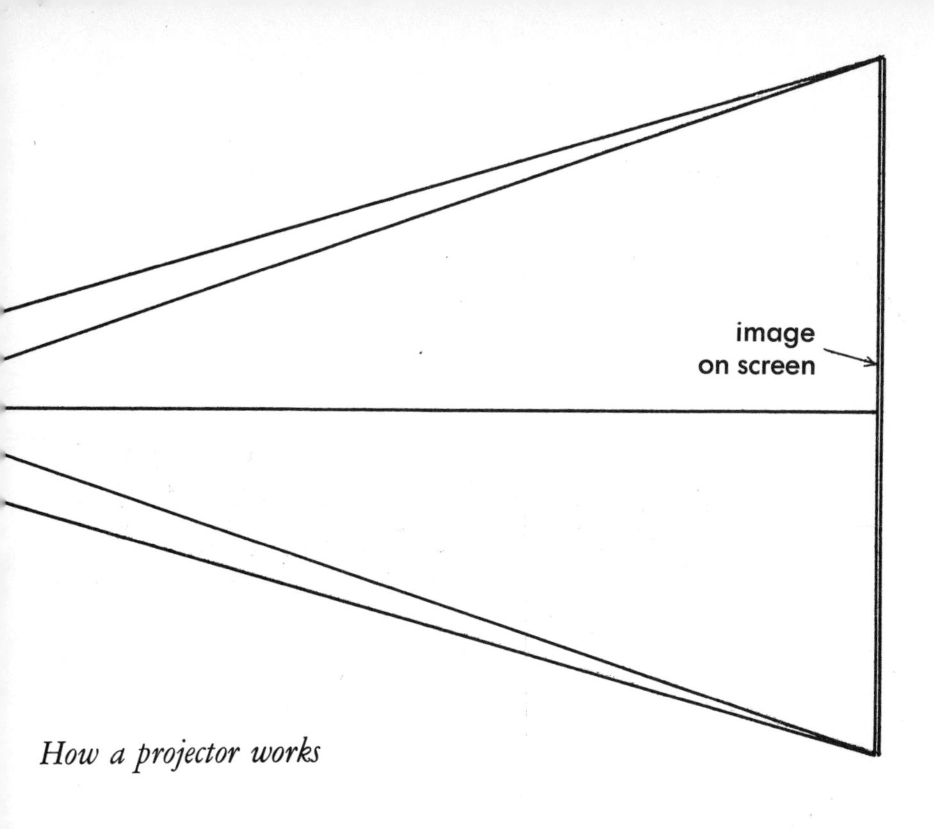

How a projector works

near the lens and the image appears at a distance on a large screen. The slide is placed in the lantern, and a powerful light is sent through it. This light first passes through two plano-convex lenses, then through the slide or film, and on through a double convex lens which projects the picture upside down onto a screen. Since the screen is at a distance from the projecting lantern, the image is very large.

CONCAVE
VE
C
VEX

The lens can be adjusted for various distances from the screen and, of course, all slides are put in the lantern upside down so that they are projected right side up.

Unlike the double convex lens, the double concave lens does not form any real image in space. Just as the double convex lens is used as a magnifying or reading glass, so the double concave is used as a reducing glass, since when you look through it you see everything much smaller. This is because all rays that do not pass through the center of the lens are bent upward toward the thicker part of the lens, and all rays that pass through the center are straight and unbent. At the point where the two rays meet, a virtual image is formed which is right side up and greatly reduced in size.

The lenses we have been discussing are the simplest kind, but all the many kinds of lenses we use are concave or convex or combinations of them. Because of them we are able to see, or if our eyes are weak, to see better. Today, opticians can produce eyeglasses to correct almost any kind of defective vision. Lenses in microscopes are used to combat disease; telescopic lenses make it possible for us to study the stars and planets. Other lenses are of utmost importance in surveying, map-making, and building construction. And still others make it possible for us to record our memories in photographs or to enjoy an evening at the movies.

Some lenses are very small—so tiny you can hardly see them; others are as much as forty inches wide. But the most amazing and wonderful lens of all is still that tiny gelatin lens in the human eye.

5 6 7 8 9 10 68 67 66 65 64 63 62